The Enchanted Kingdom

6 Original Pieces by Naoko Ikeda

Welcome to the Enchanted Kingdom. Nobody really knows where it is, but I'm quite sure you will find your way. If you don't own a wizard's wand, don't worry. With just your fingers and a piano, you can create beautiful magic.

Naoko Ikeda

ISBN 978-1-4803-5098-4

WILLIS MUSIC

Exclusively Distributed By

HAL•LEONARD®
CORPORATION
7777 W. BLUEMOUND RD. P.O. BOX 13819 MILWAUKEE, WI 53213

Visit Hal Leonard Online at
www.halleonard.com

Floating Flowers

Vibrant flowers drift softly, painting patterns in the breeze.

Naoko Ikeda

Castle in the Clouds

**The clouds in the kingdom turn different colors every day.
On very special days, they become a rainbow!**

Naoko Ikeda

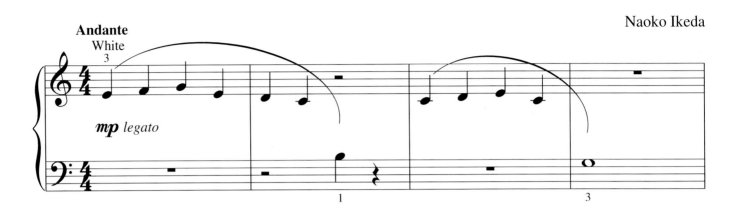

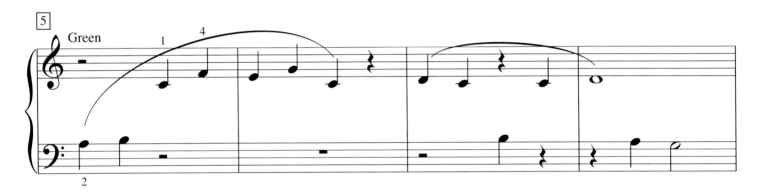

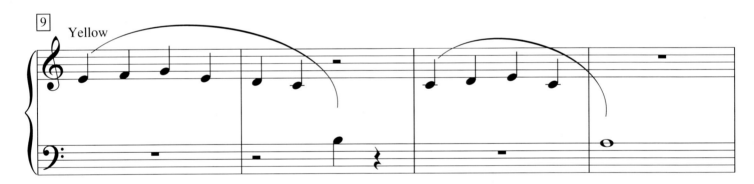

Accompaniment (Student plays one octave higher than written.)

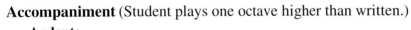

6

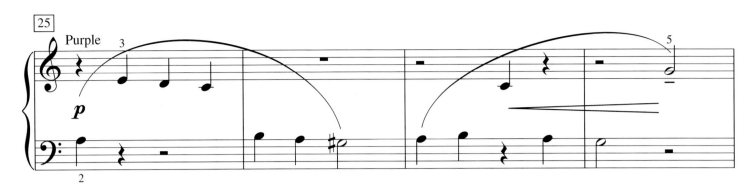

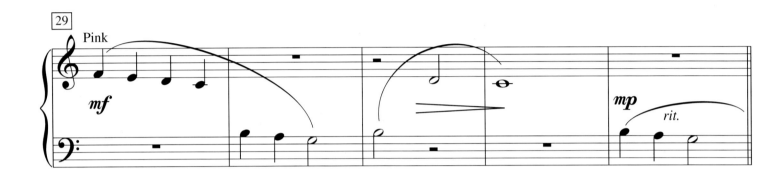

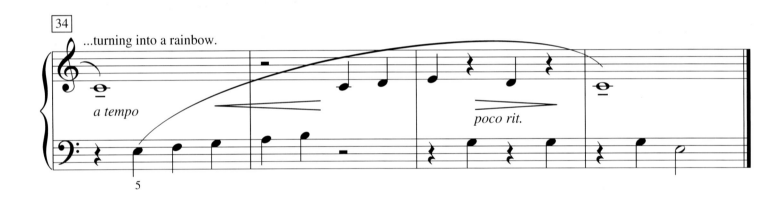

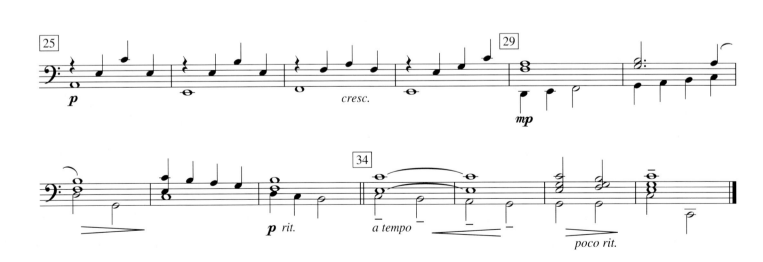

The Wizard's Wand

**In a secret room below the castle, a wizard
practices spells with his new wand.**

Naoko Ikeda

Accompaniment (Student plays one octave higher than written.)

The Playful Unicorn

**A baby unicorn plays for the first time
in a garden of floating flowers.**

Naoko Ikeda

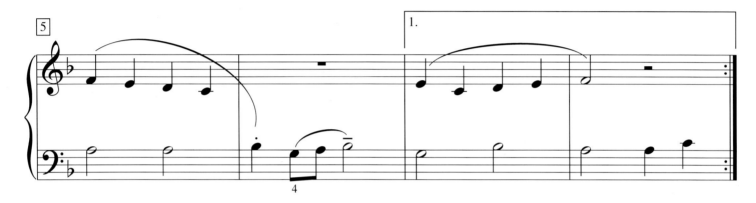

Accompaniment (Student plays one octave higher than written.)

Royal Waltz

Tonight, there is a grand ball in the castle.
Let's all dance together with the King and the Queen.

Naoko Ikeda

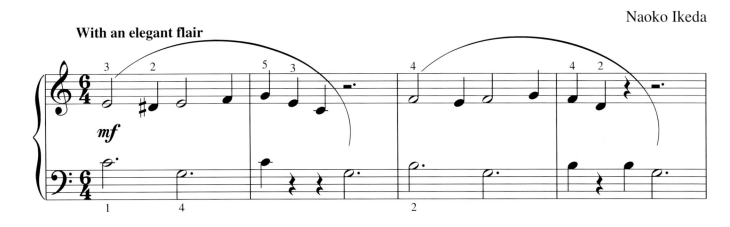

Accompaniment (Student plays one octave higher than written.)

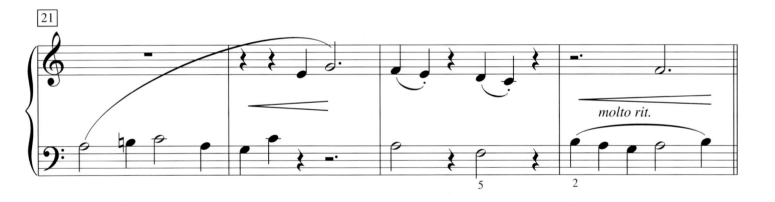

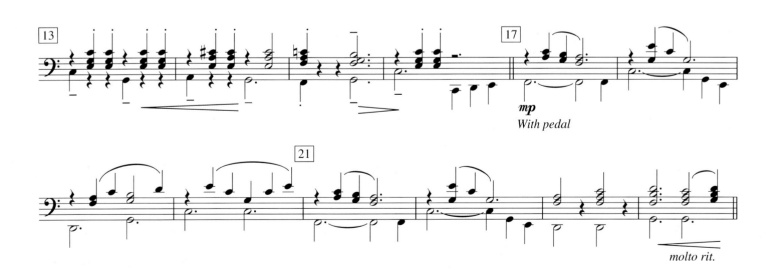

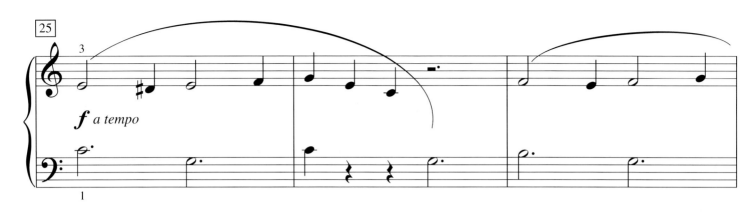

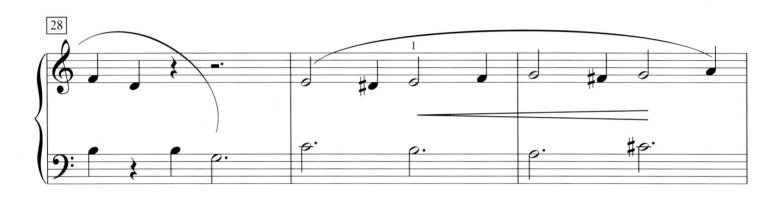

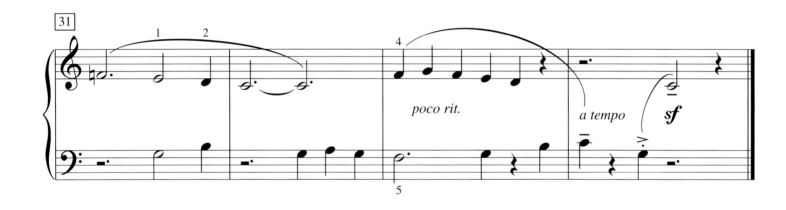

The Enchanted Kingdom

**As a magical twilight falls on the kingdom,
the Sun and Moon look down and sing a tender lullaby.**

Naoko Ikeda

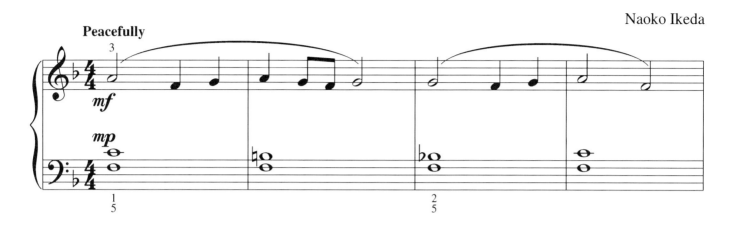

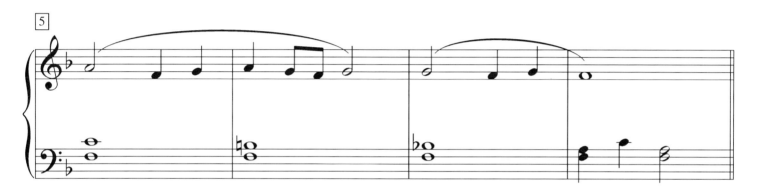

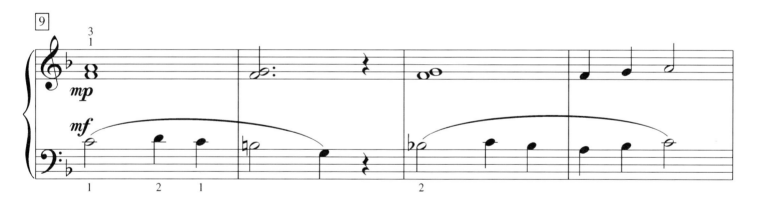

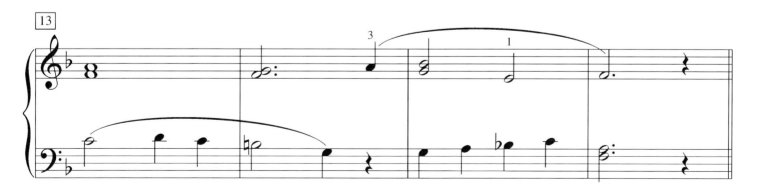

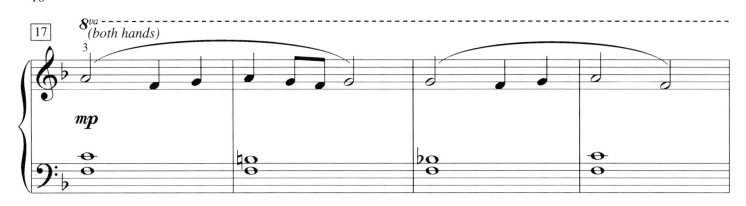

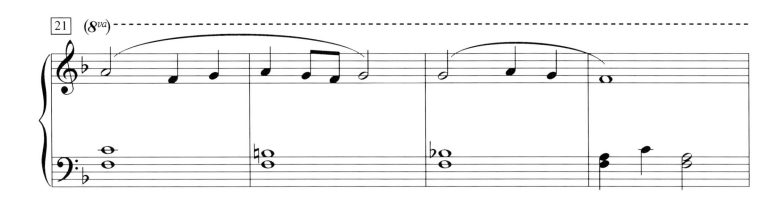

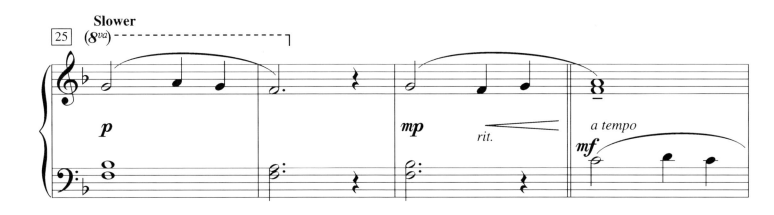

The kingdom sleeps.